Lessons from
Ignatius Loyola

David L. Fleming SJ

Review for Religious
St. Louis, Missouri
2005

Acknowledgment

The publisher gratefully acknowledges the use of Ignatius pictorial representations from the CD *Ars Jesuitica*, The Institute of Jesuit Sources, 2000.

The publisher also acknowledges permission to use the paraphase of the prayer *Soul of Christ* from David L. Fleming SJ, *The Spiritual Exercises of St. Ignatius: A Literal Translation and A Contemporary Reading*, The Institute of Jesuit Sources, 1978.

The quoted material from the *Spiritual Exercises* is taken from David L. Fleming SJ, *Draw Me Into Your Friendship*. The Institute of Jesuit Sources, 1996.

Review for Religious
3601 Lindell Boulevard
St. Louis, Missouri 63108

ISBN 0-924768-12-6

Contents

3

— ❧ —

Soul of Christ

Jesus, may all that is you flow into me.

May your body and blood
be my food and drink.

May your passion and death
be my strength and life.

Jesus, with you by my side
enough has been given.

May the shelter I seek
be the shadow of your cross.

Let me not run from the love
which you offer,

But hold me safe from the forces of evil.

On each of my dyings
shed your light and your love.

Keep calling to me until that day comes

When, with your saints,
I may praise you forever. Amen.

—David L. Fleming SJ

*This prayer is a contemporary paraphrase of the Anima Christi—a
favorite prayer of St. Ignatius which he placed at the beginning of
his book of spiritual exercises. He frequently suggested that the
retreatant conclude a prayer period by reciting this prayer.*

4

Introduction

Ignatius Loyola, author of the *Spiritual Exercises*, once described himself as being taught by God as if he were a schoolboy. At the time he was thirty years old. His *Exercises* book is the result of the lessons he was taught by God.

In sharing these lessons with us, Ignatius enters us into a way of relating to God and to others and to our world that merits the identification of a spirituality that bears his name—an Ignatian spirituality. There are a number of spiritualities in the Christian tradition, usually being passed down to us through the extraordinary graces given to an individual. We know of Benedict and the family of Benedictine spiritualities. We are familiar with Francis of Assisi and Franciscan spirituality. And we could name Teresa of Avila and Francis de Sales and many more. All Christian spiritualities find their center in Jesus, but how they experience, understand, and practically live out that relationship is what gives us the many spiritualities in the Christian tradition.

The short essays that make up this book are meant to give us a taste of Ignatian spirituality. Some repetition of themes or topics—typical of a lesson plan—is deliberately reflected in these articles both in order to emphasize Ignatius's key elements and in order to make clear the harmony among these elements. Each article acts as a short lesson about our experience and our understanding of our relationship with Jesus in the Ignatian perspective. That relationship shapes our prayer, our choices, our ministries—as Ignatius would say, "our whole way of proceeding."

The majority of the articles collected here were published over several years in the *Jesuit Bulletin*, a magazine of the Jesuits of the Missouri Province. The last three essays on Ignatian Spirituality and Educating are derived from a presentation made to faculty members at Saint Louis University in a 2003 symposium. Many of these articles also received publication in a differently edited form in *Ignis*, an Ignatian Spirituality quarterly, published in India.

As Jesus reminds us, our greatest glory is being his disciples. He will always be our Teacher. May the graces given to Ignatius Loyola be reflected for us in these lessons.

David L. Fleming SJ

6

What Are the Spiritual Exercises?

Ignatius Loyola lived during a great period of mysticism in the church. He is a contemporary of Teresa of Avila and John of the Cross, two famous Carmelite saints—all of them living in 16th-century Spain. These three people are ranked among some of the greatest saint-mystics in the church tradition. Yet many would be surprised to learn that Ignatius is a mystic.

Ignatius did not have great visions the way Teresa and John did, and he did not write any books about the paths of mystical prayer. His own mystical experience seemed to deal more with insight, the experience of "Oh, I see," when something becomes evidently clear to us. Ignatius saw how God is involved with his world and with each one of us. His vision of God working with creation and inviting each of us to labor with Jesus changed his life. Ignatius tried to share that vision and enable others to enter into it through his book the *Spiritual Exercises*.

An Exercise Book

The *Spiritual Exercises* is a book that has been in print for 450 years and has been translated into most of the world's major languages. What is odd about the *Spiritual Exercises* is that, although it is a book, we cannot pick it up and read it. That is due to the fact that it is what its very title proclaims: it is an "exercise" book.

If we have had any experience with an English or math exercise book from our grade school days, we know that we also had to have a content book which was central to the class matter. Then the accompanying exercise book called forth an active use of the material from the content book. In a similar kind of way, Ignatius wrote an exercise book. Like any exercise book, the one who uses it has to have another source for the content.

Ignatius started putting his little book together in 1522 from his own note-taking that he made as he reflected on his experiences of how he perceived God leading him in his life. In the midst of his conversion experience, he spent eleven months in a little town called Manresa in Spain, praying and working with God. He described God as one who taught him like a schoolboy.

It was during this reflective time in Manresa that Ignatius had some of his most illuminative mystical experiences. Although years later he related some of these experiences in a book called his *Autobiography*, there are no references found in his more famous book, *Spiritual Exercises*. Rather, his experiences influenced the way he wrote down exercises which would allow us to explore and grow in our own relationship with God and God's call and guidance in our lives.

25 Years of Notes

Ignatius discovered very early on through his conversations with others that the notes which he had made on his own experiences proved to be helpful to them As he kept working with men and women in their desires to grow in a relationship with God, he would nuance, correct, or add to his own notes.

Eventually—over a 25-year period—these notes became the book, *Spiritual Exercises*. When the book was printed in 1548, Ignatius kept all 500 copies. He would give the book only to a person who had gone through the prayer experiences of the Exercises, most often with the help of Ignatius, and who was now giving the Exercises to another.

Adapted to the Individual

Ignatius's concern was that the person who was going to give these Exercises to another had a sense of how to adapt them to that individual. Just as the book cannot be read, so what is also special about the book is that Ignatius presumes that only a person who has truly had the experience of the Exercises could he helpful in adapting the book for another.

This notion of adaptation is reinforced by the fact that the book does not start with a chapter one. It begins with a series of "helps" for the one who is going to be using the book in working with another. The "helps" are all hints or reminders about adapting the Exercises because God works with each individual in unique ways.

Even though the person using the Exercises book has already had the experience, Ignatius was concerned that the person might say, "God worked with me this way; therefore God must work with you in the same way." But it is an Ignatian principle that God works intimately with each one of us. And so the whole of the Exercises book structure is always to be seen in terms of adaptation.

Invited into a World Charged with Grandeur

Although there are Ignatian retreats of three days and five days and eight days, why did Ignatius identify 30 days for the full experience of the Exercises? Right from the beginning of the book's publication. Ignatius was questioned about his choice of 30 days. Some church officials pointed out that the 40 days of Lent, the 50 days of the Pentecost season, and the nine days in novenas were common numbers in the Christian tradition. Thirty days seemed to have no precedent. Ignatius said simply, "I have dealt with a lot of people, and it works."

For more than 400 years, the 30-day retreat experience of the Spiritual Exercises has been effective in countless lives in the Christian community. As Ignatius first said from his own experience, the Spiritual Exercises "work" in a time period of some 30 days.

A major grouping of people for whom Ignatius wrote the *Spiritual Exercises* are those who want to come to a decision about the direction of their lives. Do I want to marry—and whom? Do I want to stay single? Do I want to become a religious or a priest? Do I want to spend my life in church service in a foreign country?

Perhaps the decision is more about a life style than a life choice. Do I choose to live a simple life style? Do I want to align myself more with a communal life? But Ignatius also had people in mind who wanted to reform or make some changes in the way of life that they were living. They, too, find themsleves touched with their need for God and directed in their choices through the methodology of the Exercises.

A common experience today for a growing number of people is to make the Spiritual Exercises retreat in the context of their everyday life and commitments, Many people cannot take 30 days off and go to a retreat house. In his own day, Ignatius knew that people had jobs and responsibilities and could little afford the time or expense for the full 30-day experience away.

Within the series of helps that begin the book, Ignatius noted that there are various ways of making the Exercises, even in their entirety. He suggests, then, the possibility of the retreat being extended over some months, perhaps even a year. The retreat would proceed in the orderly method which Ignatius outlines, with an hour or so given to formal prayer every day. A meeting with the one giving the Exercises might occur every week instead of the every day expectation of the concentrated 30-day experience.

What is the end result of the *Spiritual Exercises?* Is there an ending to this book? Neither the book nor the retreat experience has a conclusion. Remember that it is an exercise book. Should we ever stop exercising physically or spiritually?

Having made the Spiritual Exercises, a person can say, "I have reached a certain point in my journey, and I have a sense that this is the direction that God would continue to have me go. I feel encouraged and strengthened in my journey with God." Ignatius intends that we experience God's active presence and laboring in life and in creation. He also helps us to realize our readiness to respond to God's invitation to labor with Christ "for the greater glory of God."

Ignatius wants us to live in a world filled with God's love and for us to be expressions of God's love in our everyday world. And so Ignatius invites us through the Spiritual Exercises into the experience of that same vision which he had: a world charged with the grandeur and love of God.

11

Still on the Road to Damascus: Responding to God's Dreams for Us

We know quite well the story of Jesus' call to Saul while he was on the road to Damascus. There are three accounts of this "call story": Acts 9:1-19; Acts 22:3-16; and Acts 26:2-18. The repetition of this "call of Christ" story three times in Luke's second book alerts us to the importance of such a call story for all of us, Jesus' followers, no matter when we live.

Two questions are at the heart of the story. I want to paraphrase and generalize the questions. Saul had asked the question: "Who are you—whom I am persecuting?"

12

But the basic question is: "Who are you in relation to me?" And the second question that Saul asks I might express as "What would you have me do?" As we can see, the questions refer first to a relationship and then to the action that flows or results from such a relation-ship—what would you have me do? All three stories of Saul's call by Christ emphasize that the relationship and the behavior or action are intertwined.

The Story of Saul

Like all of us, Saul had certain dreams for his life. As a Pharisee, he had the Harvard education of his day, sitting at the feet of Gamaliel, the most reputable rabbi-teacher at the time. Saul had already established for him-self a certain fame for his intellectual abilities and for his zeal in defending the Jewish religion. In our own day Saul would easily have been one of the major players in the Jewish Anti-Defamation League. Saul seemed to have received a title like "special prosecutor"—one designated to investigate, track down, and bring to justice all those disturbers in the synagogues who were preaching in the name of Jesus the Nazorean. Did he dream of himself in a role like the Judges raised up by God in olden days? Or did he fantasize himself more like one of the prophets, preaching the purity of the worship of the one God? He was a driven man, not content to work just in Jerusalem, but moving out to other cities in his zeal to do what he felt necessary and right in defending his reli-gion and eliminating troublemakers.

God worked with this human being, Saul, with all his dreams and drives. But through his relationship with Jesus, Saul-now-become-Paul was transformed. His call first of all was to listen. He was struck with a blindness about where he should go and what action he should take, and he had to be led by others. In a new way he

13

had to exercise a constancy in his prayer, listening to God and listening also to others in the community. Paul remained a man of dreams, with unflagging zeal and a drivenness now empowered by the Spirit. By God's desire, Paul was still to be teacher and he was still to be a man on a mission, now to be known as the apostle to the gentiles. What a paradox: this Jewish people's Jew, a Jew par excellence, would be identified among all the first apostles as the one prepared and dedicated by God to the evangelizing of the non-Jewish peoples. Paul could never have dreamed this dream by himself. By his patient listening to the calls of Christ in his life, Paul was entering into God's dreams for him.

The Story of Ignatius Loyola

Let us consider another follower of Christ. Many of us are familiar with the story of Ignatius Loyola. He, too, was a man of dreams. In the early years of the 16th century, he dreamed of being a chivalrous knight, at the behest of a king and perhaps at the service of a great lady. His training within the royal court only fired his dreams of somehow doing great things. A newly united Spain had just been accomplished through the royal marriage of Ferdinand and Isabella. "This land is our land" was the victorious cry of the Spanish peoples claiming back their lands from the Moors. This was the Spain which was sending forth its explorers—like Christopher Columbus—and claiming new world territories never before charted. The times might be compared to the new world of space travel opening up in our own day; it appeared to be a whole new beginning, a new day dawning, dreams only waiting to be realized. Before such grandiose visions, in an all-too-real, nitty-gritty battle between some Spanish and French forces over the city of Pamplona, Ignatius's dreams along with

14

his leg were shattered. This incident started him down his Damascus road. His recovery time back in his home castle at Loyola allowed him to read, not the romance novels which had previously fed his dreams and which were his thwarted first choice, but a book on the life of Christ and a book on saints' lives. These books became part of a questioning voice for him, similar in effect to the voice which Paul heard on the road. Ignatius continued to dream, but now his dreams were for doing great things not for a human king but for Christ. In his pondering he thought that, if Francis of Assisi and Dominic could do great things for God, why not himself?

Again we can appreciate how God uses the dreams and drives and ambitions within our human makeup and transforms them by his grace. Ignatius, like Paul, would need to be taught. He said of his Manresa experience that God taught him like a schoolboy (he was in his thirties). His favorite designation for himself at this time of his life was the word *pilgrim*. His Damascus road would take a number of years of traveling here and there, first to the Holy Land and then back to Spain and to a number of Spanish cities, such as Barcelona, Alcalá, and Salamanca, before finally settling in Paris for eight university years, and then finally Rome for the last nineteen years of his life—all of this, so that God could realize divine dreams within Ignatius.

The Ignatian Call of the King

In the *Spiritual Exercises*, Ignatius proposes an exercise entitled the Call of the King (often referred to in a shorthand kind of way as the Kingdom Meditation). It is an exercise which embodies much of what we have seen in reflecting on the calls of Christ in the lives of Paul and Ignatius. It is an exercise about dreams. Ignatius couches it in terms of a story of a human king calling for a crusade. It reflects the dream which first fired him, but it is a dream that is persistent in the epics and stories of our many human cultures. It is the stuff of which our human dreams are made.

As Ignatius presents it, this myth-story was meant to help us understand the gospel story. Jesus has a dream; it is God's dream. And Jesus calls to every man and woman and child to enter into that dream with him. And bringing our life-dreams into the dream of Jesus, we will find how we are to use all the talents and drives and passions that are God's gifts to us and let God transform them in ways that we never could have dreamed. Ignatius clearly presents to us the double aspect involved in the call of Christ. Jesus calls each one of us to a special relationship with him and, in and through that special relationship, to work with him for the reign of God by "being busy about the kingdom." In the exercise on the Call of the King, Ignatius has us reflect on our dreams, our goals, our life-desires. Like Paul and like Ignatius, we need to look at our dreams in terms of Who is Jesus for us? What place does Christ have in our life? What is our relationship to Jesus and how does it affect our way of thinking and dreaming? Have we considered Jesus' dreams about the reign of God and his invitation to us to be with him and labor with him?

As we consider this Ignatian exercise of the Call of Christ, we may find it helpful to take some reflection time with our own dreams, whatever they may be. Remember that Jesus invites all of us to be with him—to be with him in being "busy about the kingdom." It is a matter of listening to God's calls and of our responding. We are always on our own road to Damascus.

As Ignatius expresses it:

Those who are of great heart and are set on fire with

zeal to follow Jesus, eternal King and Lord of all, will not only offer themselves entirely to labor for such a mission, but will act against anything which would make their response less total. They would want to express themselves in words such as these:

> "Eternal Lord and King of all creation, humbly I come before you. Knowing the support of Mary, your mother, and all your saints, I am moved by your grace to offer myself to you and to your work. I deeply desire to be with you in accepting all wrongs and all rejections and all poverty, both actural and spiritual— and I deliberately choose this, if it is for your greater service and praise. If you, my Lord and King, would so call and choose me, then take and receive me into such a way of life."

> – from *Draw Me Into Your Friendship:*
> *A Contemporary Reading of the Exercises of St. Ignatius*
> by David L. Fleming SJ

17

Ignatian Noting

Certain moments in our life stand out for being times when God has touched us very strongly. At the time of his convalescent recovery from a cannonball-shattered leg, Ignatius Loyola had that experience. For him it was the beginning of a life's journey, a journey that included the writing of a small retreat manual called the *Spiritual Exercises*, the founding of a religious order called the Society of Jesus, and an approach to living a Christian life that we now call Ignatian spirituality.

I associate certain simple, ordinary words with Ignatius. He uses simple words, but gives them profound meaning. The simple word that I associate with the very beginning of Ignatius's conversion period is the word noting or noticing. Ignatius is a very observant man, both of events around him and of movements within his own spirit. He "notices." But more than just noticing, he "takes notice," or "notes" them. For Ignatius, to note

18

means to be aware, to pay attention, and perhaps to jot observations down in a diary. When we read today, we may sometimes use a highlighter to note lines in a text. Similarly, Ignatius recalls in his *Autobiography* that he copied some things from books in red (for Christ) and blue (for Mary). At other times he just "notes." But noting the movements within his own spirit lays the foundation for his stress on the daily examen or examination of conscience. *Noting* is why Ignatian spirituality is known as a "reflective" spirituality, that is, a spirituality for reflective people. *Noting* also is the Ignatian basis for coming to understand a language of God within us, which we call traditionally a "discernment of spirits." Ignatius is known as one of the great Christian teachers about the discernment of spirits, and it all begins in a simple way in the "noting" that became part of his experience during his recovery.

At this time he asked for romance novels to read— novels of love and adventure, the most popular printed books of the time (and of our time too, as the bookracks in our supermarkets suggest). But the only books available in the house were a life of Christ and a book of stories about saints. These two books stimulated Ignatius's thinking about his relationship with God and his own life direction. He began "noting" how God dealt with him— within, that is, in his head and heart, and without, that is, through the people and events in his everyday life.

Finding God

Who, then, is the God we struggle "to seek and to find" in our everyday life experience? Ignatius eventually summed up his approach—where we begin—in a spiritual exercise called the Principle and Foundation.

What is our principal and foundational image of God—one with which we are always meant to live? What

19

have we noticed about God? It is the Christian belief that our Trinitarian God is a God of Love. St. John bluntly says, "God is Love." But perhaps that statement sounds too abstract or too static. We might better say that God is Love loving. Ignatius's picture of God is One who is actively gifting us—Love loving. God loves, and so God creates, and God continues to gift. God's love is not something we earn or buy, wheedle or plead for. God's love is first a given, and is "unconditional."

God does not say, "If you do such and such, I will love you." God does not say, "I will love you only if you kill your firstborn," or "I will love you only if you go to Lourdes," or even "I will love you only if you keep my commandments." God is always Love loving or a Giver gifting. That really is the image that Ignatius is checking to see if we are "noting." That is our foundational image of God, the God we live with.

Giver of Gifts

Because we believe in a God of unconditional love, then it follows that the choices we make in life are all about our seeking and finding the Giver of these gifts, which reflect him. If some gifts seem to lead us away from God, no matter how good the gift, we decide that these gifts are not helpful to us and so we turn away from them. Ignatius indicates that our behavior follows upon our grasp that God loves us into existence. God loves us from the beginning, no conditions attached. Knowing that we are God's beloved, we desire to behave in ways like God. There is a great difference between seeing a face of God who loves us only on condition that we do or act in such a way and seeing the face of God who loves us unconditionally, and as a consequence we want to act—to respond—in a loving way.

When we truly drink in deeply that God loves us as

we are, then we realize that our life is not a time of testing. Lovers do not test. Our life is a time of growing and maturing. As St. Paul describes it, we mature in Christ as a baby proceeds from nursing on mother's milk to eventually eating solid food. We grow in our responsibility to make choices as God's loved ones.

When we live in God's unconditional love, this world is hardly a valley of tears. Rather, we see a world of God's gifting. But God's loved creation does cry out for us to act with God to bring it to a fulfillment and so to bring about the "kingdom of God," a reign of justice and love. We humans often obscure a world of God's gifts by wasting them, polluting them, hoarding them, destroying them. So it is not the world of gifts that is questionable; it is the human use of God's gifts—as Ignatius would have us note.

Can we be so pessimistic as to think that God in his gifting us will be defeated by our bad use of his gifts? No, God came into his creation in a definitive way in Jesus Christ. With the defining life, death, and resurrection of Jesus, God has entered all of us into the assured victorious struggle against every limiting factor, whether physical, psychological, or spiritual.

All of this way of thinking is included in the words of the Ignatian Principle and Foundation. We are seeing the face of our Christian God. This God is the God of unconditional Love—the face of God most basic to our living life. God as Love loving is truly our principle and foundation.

Who is the God to whom we relate? What kind of face does God have for us? May Ignatius help us in our noting and, as a result, in our seeking and finding God.

21

— ᧰᧰ —

Principle and Foundation

God who loves us creates us and wants to share life with us forever. Our loving response takes shape in our praise and honor and service of the God of our life.

All the things in this world are also created because of God's love, and they are the gifts presented to us so that we can know God more easily and make a return of love more readily.

As a result, we show reverence for all the gifts of creation and collaborate with God in using them, so that by being good stewards we develop as loving persons in our care for God's world and its development. But if we misuse any of these gifts of creation or, on the contrary, make them the center of our lives, we break our relationship with God and hinder our growth as loving persons.

In everyday life, then, we must hold ourselves in balance before all created gifts, insofar as we have a choice and are not bound by some responsibility. We should not fix our desires on health or sickness, wealth or poverty, success or failure, a long life or a short one. For everything has the potential of calling forth in us a more loving response to our life forever with God.

Our only desire and our one choice should be this: I want and I choose what better leads to God's deepening life in me.

– from *Draw Me Into Your Friendship:*
A Contemporary Reading of the Exercises of St. Ignatius
by David L. Fleming SJ

22

Ignatian Imagining

During his convalescence at Loyola castle, Ignatius hoped to read medieval romances about knights doing chivalrous deeds and the idealized ladies that inspired them. Perhaps such works were considered too frivolous, and none were available. He had to satisfy himself with the only two books he could get his hands on, a life of Christ and a book on the saints.

Ludolph of Saxony, a Dominican who later became a Carthusian, wrote the life of Christ. It was a popular book, in four volumes, having been translated and printed in Spain around 1503. For Ignatius this book provided his entrance into and knowledge of the Gospels; it acted as a doorway to a place where he could meet Jesus. Ignatius had very good penmanship, and he took notes from this book, writing in red ink the words of Christ and in blue

23

ink the words of Our Lady Mary. This was the beginning of the 300-page notebook that he would later treasure.

The other book was the *Flos Sanctorum*, or Lives of the Saints, by a Dominican, Jacob de Voragine. It was translated into Spanish, with a prologue by a Cistercian monk, Gauberto Vagad. This popular medieval work was also known as *Aurea Legenda*, sometimes transliterated as the Golden Legend, more literally, "golden things to be read." These stories of the saints were written with a mixture of facts and legends that were passed down through the centuries. The saints, idealized as heroes and heroines, were dramatically pictured performing miraculous deeds, all done in their following of Christ.

These two books—Ludolph's conflation of the Gospels, emphasizing the words and deeds of Jesus, and Voragine's picturesque lives of the saints, fed Ignatius's imagination even better than the tales of chivalry he had read in the past. In fact, he started noting or observing that, in his daydreams and imaginings about his life after this convalescent period, something different was happening inside him. He would dream of being a hero in service of the Spanish king, and after his initial excitement he was left feeling unsatisfied and craving for more. But when he imagined following Jesus and serving God, in the manner of the saints in Voragine's book, he felt a sense of deep satisfaction, joy, and enthusiasm that stayed with him. Ignatius was living through the period of his spiritual journey that he would later identify as the process of "discerning" how God works with us.

Contemplating

Ignatius challenges us to use our imagination in the spiritual exercises he developed. Contemplation is integral to Christian spirituality and other religious traditions. Usually this form of prayer refers to a "gazing at" or a "resting in" the divine presence. Centering prayer is a contemporary approach to this traditional form of contemplation. But when Ignatius asks us to contemplate, he is pointing us to use all our imaginative powers to enter as fully as we can into the incidents (or "mysteries" as he calls them) of the Gospels.

In the Exercises, Ignatius proposes two ways of imaginatively entering into contemplation. An example of the first approach occurs when we follow his suggestions in praying the mystery of the Incarnation/Annunciation, which is the first contemplation of the Second Week of his *Spiritual Excercise*. Ignatius asks us to take our stance with God—loving, compassionate, understanding—and to see the activities and condition of humankind from God's eternal perspective, at the moment when God becomes incarnated into human history.

An example of the second approach occurs when we follow his suggestions in praying the mystery of Jesus' nativity. Here he asks us to imagine ourselves completely present at this historic moment. We are to look at what we see, we are to listen to what we hear, we are to observe with a keen and sensitive heart all that goes on. We might even insert ourselves as a participant within this mystery, so truly are we present.

Some people have suggested that this kind of contemplation is not their gift. They believe they are just not very imaginative. Perhaps TV and video screens have dulled their own creative powers. Maybe they have more of a scientific, factual bent. However that might be, I would respond by asking if they had ever told a story. They typically have told stories about their own experiences to others. I would suggest that they just tell the Gospel story to themselves. When they tell the story, what do they see, what do they hear, what takes place? I think that many people might find entering into Ignatian

25

contemplation easier than they thought if they just remember how they tell a story.

Our daydreams—dreams of the shape of our ideals, our hopes, our successes—are empowered by our imagination. The early church communities remembered Jesus, and depicted him in the Gospels, as a creative, imaginative man. Jesus shares his dreams with us in his Sermon on the Mount—the kind of dreaming that Ignatius picks up on to picture Christ and his call to all of us in his Second Week meditation that we refer to as the Call of the King. All the parables that Jesus tells, all the symbolic actions he performs in feeding the multitudes, in healing the blind, and in curing the deaf involve the use of imagination. In fostering the use of our imagination in prayer, it is as if Ignatius is having us use this gift of God to find God. He offers us a path to our creator God and the action of God, and so also allows us to identify ourselves with his Son Jesus.

Knowing Jesus

Entering into the Gospel story through the use of our imagination is Ignatius's way of coming to know Jesus. Knowing Jesus, so as to love him more intimately, in order to follow him more closely is what our life is all about. For Ignatius, then, our Gospel-centered prayer to know, love, and follow Jesus is key to our growth and maturity as Christians. This kind of praying is not just a retreat-time experience. Just as the Gospel has an integral place in every Eucharist, so the Gospel familiarity with Jesus is ever present in the daily prayer of our life.

Like noting, which we have explored previously, imagining plays a most important role in Ignatian spirituality. Imagining past events as told in the Gospel opens us to the future. If we allow ourselves to enter into Christ's dreams, if we allow Christ to enter into our dreams and to shape them with his word, we will be seeking and finding God in the direction our life takes. Every time we come to pray the Gospels, let us remember how valued our telling of stories is. As we tell stories, Ignatius reminds us that we are imagining. And imagining, as a way of praying, keeps alive in us a way of knowing Jesus that was also possessed by St. Paul and the early Christian communities. Let us be grateful to Ignatius for the gift he has shared with us, the gift of imagining so as to know Jesus.

Ignatian Communicating

Communicating is an integral part of Ignatian spirituality.

In the Exercises—Ignatius's guide to the thirty-day retreat—he identifies the final prayer period with the title "Contemplation on the Love of God." Fuller translations may say "Contemplation to Obtain the Love of God," or "Contemplation to Attain the Love of God," which may be misleading—they make it sound as if we are meant to be busy in our prayer wooing God to love us, or as if we are reaching up to God to get his love. "The Contemplation on the Love of God" seems to work best.

In this final prayer period Ignatius has us review how we have seen and experienced God loving during the previous days of the retreat—all the days of the Four Weeks of the *Spiritual Exercises*. Since we can readily recall and reflect upon our experiences of God's loving, this aspect of the prayer period is meant to be truly a contemplation. But Ignatius also challenges us to enter into the ways of God's loving. Can we begin to love in all the ways that God loves, in the limitless actions of God's loving?

Once again Ignatius enters us into this reflection in a deceptively simple way. He wants us to note how love gets expressed. Ignatius observes that love expresses itself in deeds over and above words. At first we might think that Ignatius is disparaging words or verbal communication. But he goes on to describe that lovers share with each other whatever it is that each has. The Spanish word that Ignatius uses is *comunicar*. Lovers communicate, that is, share, with each other in the myriad of ways that speak out love.

Sharing and Loving

What Ignatius stresses for us is that love is all about communicating. If there is no communicating, there is no love. We well know this from experiences of Marriage Encounter, family counseling, or in today's programs of community renewal in religious life. Communicating is essential to the way of loving, the way of being Christian, the way of being a follower of Christ.

And so Ignatius asks in this final exercise that we tell ourselves stories about all the ways we have experienced God loving us during the various Weeks. This prayer period (or perhaps more than one) becomes a review of these experiences. Having been reminded by Ignatius that lovers share (communicate), what do we say or do as we see how God communicates his love to us?

We probably are familiar with the prayer that Ignatius suggests as a response to this love. It is a prayer original to him called "Take and Receive." It is a lover's prayer that communicates the desire to share what we have with

29

God. It is hard to name what we want to share that is not already a gift from God. Sharing gifts given is wonderful, but what, if anything, do we have to share with God that God does not have?

The brilliance of Ignatius's prayer is his pinpointing our unique gifts to God: "our" liberty, the potential of freedom since God invites and realizes true freedom for us as we exercise this very potenial; "our" memories, which God does not have without our sharing them; "our" understandings, crazy and limited though they may be, but God does not have them without our sharing them; "our" choices, whether of friendships or music or flavor of ice cream, we can share with God. As a lover, I don't give up or give away anything—I do not give up my memory, or my liberty, or my choices. No, as a lover, I share with the one I love.

Divine Loving

To stimulate our own way of praying, let us look at some of the ways that Ignatius recalls how God loves us. In his first point, Ignatius would have us look at all the gifts that God has given to us—the gifts of our life, our family, our friends, perhaps husband or wife or religious community, our talents and education, our native country and the times in which we live, our faith, our church, the forgiveness of our sin, and the promise of life forever with God.

In his second point, Ignatius focuses us on how God is not content with just giving us gifts, but gives us himself as well in Jesus, his only Son. Jesus not only gives himself to us in his life, passion, and death, but continues to be consoler for us in his resurrected life. Jesus gifts us with his being our food and drink in the Eucharist. Jesus puts himself in our hands and allows us to be his hands and his feet and his voice in our world. God holds nothing back.

30

In his third point, Ignatius focuses us on the effort and struggle that God continues to exercise in his love for us. God is not a distant, snap-of-the-finger miracle God. Our God is a God who labors over his creation, who labors in Jesus to be born, to be exiled, to live in an occupied country, to be an itinerant preacher, to be betrayed, to be put to death, to be raised up. It is the laboring God that we have particularly experienced in the Third Week. This is a God who labors with his church, with all the religious belief systems, somehow all working to a realization of God's reign. To see God is to see One laboring in love. Jesus even used as an image for God a woman in labor, struggling, but then finding joy in bringing forth new life. I have sometimes called this Ignatian image of God a "busy God." Our creator and redeeming God is involved in a labor of love.

In his fourth point, Ignatius stresses the limitless action of God's love. God has broken through even the apparently hopeless limit of death in giving back to Jesus not only his life but also gifting him with his death. Jesus wears the marks of his death forever in his risen life. So, too, for all of us, death will become only one more gift of God, restored to us in our risen life. The sun with its rays of light and heat poured forth without measure, a spring that gushes forth its waters in an inexhaustible flow, are but pale images of our God pouring out his love.

It is in reviewing these various ways of seeing and experiencing God's love showered upon us that Ignatius draws up his prayer response of the "Take and Receive." As ones who want to express our love, what can we communicate, how can we share with this loving God? Ignatius gently puts forth his prayer as one way of responding, but immediately tells us to "communicate" however it seems best for us. Communicating is everything, for, after all, lovers communicate.

We can be grateful to God for Ignatius and his sharing with us his gift of communicating, helping us to seek and find God.

— ❧ —

Take and Receive

Take, Lord, and receive all my liberty, my memory, my understanding, and my entire will — all that I have and call my own. You have given it all to me. To you, Lord, I return it. Everything is yours; do with it what you will. Give me only your love and your grace. That is enough for me.

from *Draw Me Into Your Friendship:*
A Contemporary Reading of the Exercises of St. Ignatius
by David L. Fleming SJ

32

How Do We Live an Ignatian Spirituality?

A Media God

Ignatian spirituality is sometimes called "a spirituality for busy people." Sometimes it is identified as a "worldly spirituality." At other times it is described—again quite accurately, I think—as a "world-affirming spirituality."

We need, first of all, to agree on what we mean by spirituality. Simply said, spirituality is "a way of living." In our Christian context we fill out our description by adding "influenced by the Gospels and Jesus' gift of the Spirit." In a slightly more technical description, we might say that spirituality deals with a faith vision (a way of seeing), its articulation, and its application to our everyday life with God, with our neighbor, and with our world.

How do we come to live the Christian spirituality that is identified with Ignatius Loyola, with his way of seeing God, neighbor, and world?

Most persons, as they live their lives, keep developing new ways of seeing by becoming aware of the viewpoints of others. In terms of a religious or faith vision, it may happen when we hear a homily or when we read an article or book. An influential teacher can share a vision of life, or a good friend may share deeply and effectively during a seemingly simple conversation. Ignatius Loyola shared his faith vision in his classic retreat manual called *Spiritual Exercises* and in his religious life rule called *Constitutions of the Society of Jesus*. Ignatius often made use of an expression—"our way of proceeding"—when he wrote the rule of life for the Society of Jesus. If I could expand the application of this expression beyond Jesuit life, I would observe that there is a "way of proceeding," a way of going about life, a faith-way of seeing and entering into relationship with our world which can be described as Ignatian.

It is obvious that we are not talking about some pious practices or devotions. Rather, Ignatian spirituality is more a matter of basic attitudes, ways of relating to Jesus and God the Father, certain values emphasized, and our human involvement in the work of the kingdom, the reign of God.

What are some of the pieces that make up the "way of proceeding" that we identify as Ignatian spirituality? These pieces would include the following: an understanding that God is a media God who breaks into our day in all the ways that are possible; a consistently reflective approach to our human experience which allows us to

34

be aware of God's communication with us; and a prayer method which helps us to enter imaginatively into the life of Jesus in order to come to know, love, and follow him.

A Media God

For St. Ignatius Loyola, God is a God who wants to break into our life through as many channels as our "cable TV set" has.

Today we are conscious of the importance of media—usually meaning newspapers, television, radio, movies, and now computers with internet and e-mail. Ignatius, without any foreknowledge of our modern media, imaged God as breaking into our life in a myriad of ways every day. Through people and events, through our own interior moods and affections, obviously in a privileged way through our listening to the Word of God and through our prayer, God is trying to communicate with us.

We may have had the experience of trying to communicate with someone who speaks a different language—someone who does not know or speak our native language. Often there is the tendency for us to speak louder as if there is a hearing problem rather than an understanding one. We may have an analogy here to how we pray to God. We shout "our" language of request, asking for things, perhaps demanding them. All the while God is trying to respond, and we do not even listen to or try to understand God's language.

Ignatius tries to get us to be more aware of how God enters into our everyday life. If God is a media God for Ignatius, then the following element is immediately its corollary for Ignatian spirituality.

Human Experience and Reflection

Ignatius takes us from a black-and-white-silent-movie approach to our world to a full-color richness, with sound

35

and music. He presents a picture of creation—expressed succinctly in the Principle and Foundation and in the Contemplation on the Love of God in his *Spiritual Exercises*—that makes us more conscious of the multi-layered experience in our workaday world. Our problem as people of faith is not that God is absent from our life and world. It is rather that we are so busy, so self-focused, that we do not give God a thought. Even a regular Sunday Mass experience—what is meant to be a special "sabbath" celebration with God—can become a formalized ritual and a less reflective human experience.

Ignatius observed in the Old Testament how the Israelites saw that God had been continuously present to them and had guided and comforted them in good times and in bad. Ignatius reflected on his own experience, his dreams and desires, and began to discover how God and God's desires became more apparent to him in the events of living. An essential part of Ignatian spirituality is a God who comes in many ways into our life—a true media God. That is the kind of Christian God we come to know—through a sensitized awareness. Our daily experience is important. Experiential awareness and reflection on it are central to being able to hear and respond to the language of God—to the God who uses media to communicate with us.

To Know Christ Jesus: Laboring

We often use the expression "media event" when we refer to a major newsworthy happening. The "media event" of our Christian God is God-becoming-incarnate, the person of Jesus Christ, acknowledged as Son of God, our savior.

Ignatius suggests in the *Spiritual Exercises* that we might picture the three Persons of our triune God looking upon the human scene on planet earth—much like

36

we look at our TV evening world news—and then we observe that they engage in conversation about what could be done to heal and right our human situation. Our triune God makes a choice to enter into the messiness of human living, even into its most unfair, cruel, and death-dealing aspects. The divine decision is that the second Person will become incarnate—depending upon permission from the Virgin Mary, waiting upon her fiat. And so Jesus is born of poor parents in an occupied land and knows the experience of living as a refugee.

Looking carefully and entering into the Gospel presentation of how Jesus acts and goes about life is Ignatius's "way of proceeding" for our own coming to know and love and follow Jesus. We follow the pattern that all Jesus' disciples have known since the first apostles responded to his call. Ignatius does not preach or draw moral example from the Gospels. He puts us in prayer contact with the Gospels and has us enter each scene with eyes and ears of faith and become present to the people involved. In this way of praying—called Ignatian contemplation—we drink in how Jesus looks, how he listens, how he speaks, how he acts. We learn much also from our taking in how other people in the Gospel incident interact with and respond to Jesus.

To live, St. Paul says, is "to know Christ Jesus." And Jesus says to Philip, "Philip, if you have seen me, you have seen the Father." How do we come to know Jesus, and so come to know God? For Ignatius, the one who sees and hears Jesus will begin to live the way that God's children live—the way that the Son of God lives, the One who calls God *Abba*.

A word that takes on divine meaning for Ignatius is *labor* or *work*. As Ignatius envisioned the Trinity, it was a labor of the Trinity to enter into the salvation of

37

humankind: "Let us work the redemption of the human race." From the very beginning of Jesus' life, labor was involved—no room for them in the inn, then an exile in Egypt. And the great work of redemption is accomplished by his suffering and death on the cross and his being raised by God. Jesus described his mission as a choice of labor: "My Father works, and I work" (Jn 5:17). What we begin to understand in Ignatian spirituality is that our God is a busy God. Like Jesus, our own busyness, our labor, is, then, a point of contact with, not a distancing from, our God.

38

How Do We Live an Ignatian Spirituality?
Poor in Jesus

We have been considering some of the pieces that make up the "way of proceeding" that we identify as Ignatian spirituality. We turned our attention to God as Ignatius came to know him—as a media God who breaks into our day in all the ways that are possible, a God always trying to make contact with us, a God who desires to communicate with us, a God who wants to be the God involved in our daily living.

Our way of coming to know this God is through a consistently reflective approach to our human experience. A key to this kind of reflection is given to us when we look carefully, by means of our gospel contemplation prayer, at how Jesus acts and goes about life. This prayer method becomes Ignatius's "way of proceeding" for our coming to know and love and follow Jesus.

To Know Christ Jesus: Poor

Ignatius does more than just put us into contact with Jesus as the one who enables us to live like sons and daughters of a God we too call Father. In the way that Ignatius has carefully constructed the Spiritual Exercises, he has given us his own gospel picture of Jesus. It may at first strike us as peculiar, almost heretical, to hear that Ignatius gives us his gospel picture of Jesus. Yet that is what each of our four Gospels do. Each Gospel presents a picture of Jesus—according to Matthew or Mark or Luke or John—or, perhaps more correctly, according to the memories of the early churches they represented.

Ignatius uses one adjective consistently to describe Jesus. The adjective is not loving, compassionate, gentle, or kingly—appropriate though any of these words may be. Ignatius has a predilection for the word *poor*. For Ignatius, it seems that an equivalent noun is *humility*. Humility has its Latin root in a word meaning *ground*. When we are at ground level, we have nowhere to go but up. We might well be described as poor. As Ignatius relates to Jesus, he is, above all, a humble man—one who lives "grounded." Why should this be so important?

For Ignatius, following the inspiration of St. Paul, the basic description of Jesus is rooted in an early Christian hymn quoted by Paul in his letter to the Philippians: "He did not consider godliness something to cling to, but rather he emptied himself, taking on our human nature" (Ph 2: 6-7). Jesus became poor by becoming incarnate—going from godliness to humanness, an emptying out. Jesus was born poor—lying in a stable manger, fleeing as a refugee to Egypt, living a simple workman's life in Nazareth. Jesus chose to be poor—led by the Spirit to be an itinerant preacher and teacher, having no wife or children, no place to call home. Jesus dies poor—stripped even of the clothes he wore, considered a criminal and an outcast, buried in another man's tomb. Above all, for Ignatius, Jesus is poor in that he has nothing to claim as his—everything is gift, everything is given him by his Father, even what he has to say. So Jesus is poor in himself—true humility—but rich in his gifts, especially in his identity of being the Son of God, and free in his sharing with us, as brothers and sisters of his who in his name call upon God as "Our Father."

Jesus is free—he clings to nothing. He holds fast to nothing because everything is gift. Lovers share whatever they have with those they love. Jesus—the gift of God's love—gives himself over totally to us, even allowing us to put him to death. He loves us to the very end, which means that he loves us, paradoxically, in such a way that even death presents no limit to his love. God raises him up, showing us in Jesus (like the visible sacrament he is) that God's love cannot be defeated. In his death and resurrection Jesus gifts us with our hope of risen life forever—a life of love with God. Although Ignatius closes a number of his letters with the expression "poor in goodness," the true paradox of Jesus' poverty/richness is caught in another Ignatian closing: poor in Jesus.

How Do We Live an Ignatian Spirituality?
Direction and Ministry

We have been looking at some of the characteristics that make up the "way of proceeding" we identify with Ignatian spirituality. We looked at God as Ignatius came to know him—as a God who breaks into our lives in all the ways that are possible. We also considered the ways we can come to know, love, and follow Jesus through the gospel contemplation prayer method Ignatius taught us.

We examine now another aspect of Ignatian spirituality—one that also flows from how we relate to God and from the many ways in which God works with us. Just as God worked our redemption incarnately—using human means to bring about a divine end—so Ignatius places great importance on a spiritual director or a spiritual guide as a normal means of our making progress in holiness, of our faithful following along Jesus' path.

A Spiritual Guide

A spiritual guide is something like a mirror. We all can live without a mirror, but a mirror makes combing hair, putting on makeup, or shaving a lot easier. With a mirror we do a better job of cleaning and grooming ourselves. And so a spiritual director is like a mirror. It is not so much the wisdom or great insight that this or that guide may bring to our relationship. Rather the importance of the guide is found in the careful listening, in being able to reflect back as a mirror does. Through the guide's help, we come to see how God is working in our life. We learn how apparently scattered things come together into some meaningful pattern. We even gain a little understanding of the kind of rhythm or pattern of interaction that God and we seem to form in our relationship. For Ignatius, then, a human spiritual director or guide helps us to have a consistent alertness to God's movements and arrive at a discerning interpretation of those movements for our spiritual growth. It is with the help of a spiritual guide that we learn ever better the "language of God" spoken through the various media—those uncountable vehicles of God's communication—that flood our lives. It is with the help of the spiritual director that we can begin to grow as discerning people, people whose decisions or choices are made primarily in reference to their deepening relationship with God. How does God want to work with us at this point in our life? What would God have us do now? These are questions for us as discerning people. For Ignatius, a spiritual guide is always meant to be a help, a mirror, an angel—a con-

43

sistent way that God works "sacramentally" to point out or uncover a divine pattern that is integral to our Christian understanding of God's providence affecting our lives and eliciting our response.

Ministry and Mission

There is another aspect to our active involvement with a God who is coming into our life in so many ways daily—we begin to realize that God works through us as one of his media to continue his work of bringing about the kingdom. So what we do or do not do makes a difference in the way that God can break into his own created world. In a true sense God has made himself weak and dependent on us.

Ignatius describes us as *instruments*—a word which does not please our ears today in an age of personalism and individual rights. We ought not, however, lose the beautiful spiritual truth of the idea. Ignatius wanted people to realize the great glory of being an instrument in the hands of God. Ignatius was always begging God to use him, to work with and through him. If we live an Ignatian spirituality, we feel the pulse of God in our life. We continue to desire to respond ever more whole-heartedly to the calls of God. We want to be an instrument in the hands of God. As a result, mission or ministry—working with God—in Ignatian spirituality takes on certain characteristics.

The first is from the makeup of the book *Spiritual Exercises*. This book demands that the person making the Exercises have the help of a director or guide. Whatever the ministry, we, influenced by an Ignatian spirituality, do not just do something for others, but interact with others in such a way that we involve people in the very ministry. In an "Ignatian" parish or retreat center or social work agency, collaboration—that is, a working together,

44

a working with—is the presumed "way of proceeding." Ministry demands teamwork, an interaction with others. We have a faith vision that we make a difference. God desires that we make a difference as collaborators— with him and with our fellow human beings—in bringing about the reign of God.

Finally, for us who try to live Ignatian spirituality, there is the deep-down desire to share our faith, to be evangelizers, to witness by our lives to the Good News of Jesus Christ. Whatever be our ambit of family and recreation or whatever be our line of work, we want Jesus to be central. We want Jesus to be known and to be just as real for others as he has become for us. We witness to our faith in the way we live and in the work we do. We witness to the person of Jesus and the meaning of the Gospels. We are the evangelizers whom Jesus has called "to make disciples of all nations." For, in living Ignatian spirituality, we experience the Jesus who confirms that "I am with you always, until the end of the world" (Mt 28:20).

Growing as a Contemplative-in-Action: Imagination and Contemplation

Ignatius is known as a contemplative-in-action. One of the gifts that he has shared with us who find a home in Ignatian spirituality is a way of growing in our ability to be contemplatives-in-action. For us to grow as contemplatives-in-action, I believe that it is necessary for us to focus on the aspects of Ignatian spirituality which deal with the heart. For I think that anyone trying to live Ignatian spirituality needs to approach life more through the heart than the head. The head—keeping the clarity of Ignatian vision—is important. But vision or "head" is never enough for Ignatius. For Ignatius by his personal example and through the Exercises calls us to pay attention to our hearts, our affections, our feelings.

Imagination, contemplation, and discernment are central facets of Ignatian spirituality. I believe that these three are all interconnected and that they all relate to the heart. As we consider them, we measure how healthy and vibrant is our living of Ignatian spirituality.

Imagination

One of the qualities of Ignatius's personality was that he was a romantic. He dreamed dreams. Chivalry was still in the air in sixteenth-century Spain. Ferdinand and Isabella had only recently united Spain and driven out the Moors—the Muslim occupiers of Spain for over seven hundred years. Along with that reconquest and consolidation, they also looked expansively and sponsored the Christopher Columbus exploration voyage of 1492. New worlds were opening up for the worldly as well as the heavenly kingdom. Ignatius thought of war as glorious deeds; he could dream of distinguishing himself in the service of a king and a royal lady. He could easily transfer his thoughts to the glorious deeds necessary in the conquest of Christ's enemies and the conversion of pagan peoples. Why not be a great saint like Francis or Dominic? As Jesus described greatness in the eyes of the world ("their great ones make their importance felt" (Mk 10:42), it was exactly what Ignatius envisioned—the desire for a great name and the ability to make power felt.

Even in the midst of his conversion at Loyola castle, Ignatius only changed his dreams from doing great things in the world to doing great things for God. He seems to be in a conversion process, but he remains a little romantically self-centered. He still has dreams, but now dreams of spending his life in the land where Jesus had lived—doing good things (whatever that might mean),

47

perhaps converting the Muslim occupiers of that land. We know that the Franciscan provincial in the Holy Land had to nip this self-proclaimed discernment in the bud by threatening him with excommunication.

Ignatius always remained a man of imagination. His imagination continued to give him vision, but the change seemed to come in the small practical steps that he began to take to realize the vision, or at least the direction towards the vision. This becomes apparent in his three-times-frustrated attempts to get a college degree, which on the fourth try landed him in Paris. There at the university he was successful, not so much because he became more focused or organized, but because he profited from the practicality of the Parisian method of education. This approach, so successful for Ignatius and the first companions, went on to form the basis for the practical vision enshrined in the Jesuit method of education called the *Ratio studiorum*. It directed an imaginative and practical way of educating for which Jesuit schools were famed.

Imagination and practicality also mark the way Ignatius goes about the writing of the *Constitutions of the Society of Jesus*. Their inductive structure is both visionary and practical. Although the missionary aspect of the Jesuits was always a part of the Ignatian vision, education as a ministry becomes imaginatively realized as a privileged way of renewal through the practical demands of benefactors and bishops. We need to remember from these examples of Ignatius's own life that imagination and practicality can go hand in hand. When we do some self-reflection, we might ask ourselves whether we find that in our efforts at being practical we at the same time stifle imagination in ourselves and others.

Contemplation

Ignatius's genius or gift of grace or their combination was the way he applied imagination to prayer. Ignatius came to know the Jesus of the Gospels not by a study of the Gospel text but by using imagination to enter the gospel world. He came to enjoy an intimate relationship with Jesus because he had watched Jesus' facial expression, he had listened to the resonant tone of his voice, and he had observed the loving care of his interactions with others. As Ignatius prayed for the grace to know Jesus more intimately that he might love him more and so be able to follow him more closely, he lived with Jesus in scene after scene of the Gospels. Imagination is at the heart of the way of praying called Ignatian contemplation. Perhaps we all need to nurture a little of the romantic side of ourselves, as Ignatius did, in order to stir up our imaginations.

Contemplation became the favorite way of praying for Ignatius because it left human reasoning and control behind. If we enter into imagination, we allow ourselves to be free of our usual restraints. Sometimes in a planning process it is called "blue-skying." The image of sky is an apt one since it indicates an expanse without limit. It is the imagination of a good cook who goes beyond the recipes as written in the cookbook and who creatively combines ingredients into luscious new concoctions. It is the imagination of a God who can take all the messes that we humans make and continue in God's own providence to bring creation out of chaos, life out of death.

If we enter into the Gospel scene through imagination, we allow ourselves the freedom to watch whatever takes place in the encounter, to listen to whatever is said and the way it is said, and to observe all the actions that speak so much louder than words. What we pick up through the sensitivity of our imagination-senses gives us a knowledge and intimacy with Jesus that no biblical studies could ever provide. We develop a relationship with Jesus that is as unique and personal as any of our human relationships. We know and we love Jesus. Our knowledge and our love is real; it is no longer just a language of pious devotion speaking out words of praise and love and reverence.

Imagination is key to Ignatian contemplation. Praying the Gospel incidents in the Ignatian manner provides us with the way of knowing Jesus more intimately so that we may love him more intensely and follow him closely. We are growing as contemplatives-in-action.

Growing as a Contemplative-in-Action: Contemplation and Discernment

Ignatius Loyola has presented us with a way of growing in our spiritual lives, sharing in the grace he received—the grace of being a contemplative-in-action. In the previous article we considered imagination and contemplation as central facets of Ignatian spirituality. Now we will examine how discernment is interconnected with imagination and contemplation.

Discernment

Because imagination has allowed us to come to know Jesus in a true and intimate way, we have laid the foundation for being discerning people in the way

Ignatius understands discernment. Too often we associate discernment with the listing of pros and cons on a sheet of paper, doing some praying about the matter, coming to a decision, and then standing ready to feel a sense of peace. Ignatius does identify a "third time" of choice or decision making that does involve this kind of reasoning process. But he suggests that we make use of this method when we do not find success with two previous methods or "times" he describes in his book *Spiritual Exercises*. In these first and second times, Ignatius directs that we pray to God to give us confirmation according to affective, nonrationally focused experiences.

Ignatius speaks of a "first time" of election or choice as a time in which God by his grace gives to us an undeviating clarity of direction or decision. Ignatius refers to the conversion of Saul—from persecutor to evangelizer Paul—and the call of Matthew—from tax-collector to evangelizer—as two examples of first-time discernment. Many commentators today, however, would warn us from focusing upon the extraordinary aspect of these calls. Rather we should look to the undeviating sense of call or decision that we see in both Paul's and Matthew's decision to follow Christ.

Probably we would find this sense of call or inclination not so rare or unusual in our own lives. Provided that we are not people who are always absolutely sure and clear about our decisions and directions (this might indicate presumption or pride rather than discernment), there are times when what we are to do or what direction we are to take seems to rise up inside us with undeviating clarity. For Ignatius, this is God's Spirit working within us in a "first time" discernment. Our response must be to thank God and to offer the decision or choice to God in terms of our loving service and then to act on it.

The "second time" discernment process outlined in

52

the Exercises is a key contribution of the saint and mystic Ignatius. It is based on our sensitivity to the movements that go on within our spirit. Ignatius calls these movements "spirits" and we feel the result of these spirits in our affections. Our affections—what we commonly call our feelings—give us a sense of spiritual consolation or spiritual desolation. The Ignatian description of consolation and desolation that merits the designation spiritual (*Spiritual Exercises*, Rules for Discernment [316] and [317]) must be carefully attended to if we are to become discerning people. Movements result in affections that may excite and strengthen us in our following of Christ, or they may lead us to darkness and discouragement. This "second time" discernment occurs when we are able to discern the spirits through our sensitivity to the affections being stirred in us. We might describe it as "learning the language of God."

Discernment, especially through movements of consolation and desolation, is united closely with the contemplations of the Exercises. Ignatius intends that, through these contemplations on the Gospel mysteries, we observe Jesus so closely that we drink in not only how he responds to people and events but also how he comes to decisions and choices. It is like mentoring. It is the example we drink in, even more than any teaching provided or directions given. Our absorbing Jesus' way of discerning is all part of the "following" that goes along with "knowing intimately" and "loving more," which is the grace we pray for beginning in the Second Week of the Exercises. To look at it from another perspective, we love Jesus as the center of our lives, and our discerning of choices and directions always touches back into that centering relationship. The disturbance of desolation happens because our movement is away from Jesus; the deepening of faith, hope, or love, as a movement of consolation, happens because we are enhancing our relationship with Jesus.

The "second-time" discernment, then, is intimately tied in with imagination and contemplation. For Ignatius, the way of gospel contemplation is all of a piece with becoming discerning people. Intimacy with Christ, which this kind of imaginative entering into the gospel scene allows, not only provides us with the "feel" of discernment in Jesus' life, but also makes our love-relationship with Jesus the true norm of our discernment.

Discernment in any of the Ignatian three "times" demands a certain amount of imagination, since we are dealing with possibles and futuribles—and not just working with facts and figures and what is. We need to trust our imaginations as a way that we allow God to be creative in communicating with us.

Contemplatives-in-Action

To be a contemplative-in-action means to be a discerning person. A "contemplative" is one who is somehow in touch with God; and a contemplative "in action" is one who is caught up in the choices and decisions of everyday living in relationship with God. If we are in contact with God as we continue to make our choices and decisions, we are discerning people. We may not put the two—discernment and contemplation—together in this way, but I think we find that discerning people and contemplatives-in-action are the same. In other words, discernment and contemplation are not a "sometime" activity but rather a quality of living that we strive to deepen by God's grace as we grow spiritually.

Where is our heart? Heart touches into the depth of our being. Do we value imagination as one of the doorways into these depths? Using our imaginations allows God a way into our lives that surprises and takes us unaware. Imagination allows us to approach ministry in creative ways imitative of God's creative action. Using our imaginations is the way to enter into Ignatian contemplation—a privileged way to know Jesus so that we may love him more and follow him more closely. Through our imagination and through this approach to contemplation, we find that God provides us ways to learn a divine language and become discerning people.

Where is our heart? Let us look back over how much we value and use our imaginations in our prayer, in our own discerning, and in our ministries with others. How often do we touch into the Gospels with an Ignatian approach of contemplation? Is getting to know Jesus so as to be able to live with God a constant in my life as a Christian? Is my relationship with Jesus a present and reliable norm for my discerning? Do I have a sense of growing as a discerning person? What holds me back from growing as a contemplative-in-action? What helps me to grow as a contemplative-in-action?

As we desire to grow spiritually—to grow as contemplatives-in-action—it is good for us to ask: Where is our heart? For the heart of Ignatian spirituality is to be found in our use of imagination, contemplation, and discernment.

Journeying with Ignatius the Pilgrim

Ignatius, at the request of his early companions, dictated a kind of autobiography, detailing his life-events from the Pamplona wounding and convalescent time at Loyola through his coming to Rome and the beginnings of the Society of Jesus. In the book, his favorite and consistent word for referring to himself is the *pilgrim*, a word that he adopts from the time of his spiritual experience at Manresa up to his time in Rome.

For me, there are three factors in being a pilgrim. First, a pilgrim has a destination. He or she is not just a wanderer, a vagrant. A pilgrim is going to a definite place; it has an identity. Another factor is the journey involved in the pilgrimage. The journey may have no set path; it may involve a certain meandering—all part of the trip—with the destination never out of mind. The third factor in being a pilgrim is the significance of both the journey and the destination—the implications of the journey for the one involved (the pilgrim) and the meaning of the destination.

Ignatius himself does not give us our ultimate meaning for any one pilgrimage journey, but he does reveal to us his quest for God and the direction that God gives to his life—that quest remains for each of us our own life pilgrimage. Ignatius is a pilgrim who has special meaning for us, and who, through the Spiritual Exercises, has given us a way of proceeding on our own pilgrimage.

Being a pilgrim or following a "way" is very central to Ignatian spirituality. The influence of Ludolph's Life of Christ on Ignatius cannot be ignored. Ludolph himself had stressed a word identified with pilgrimage (the Spanish *discurrir*) to describe a person who not only travels through different parts of the world but also, in reflection and prayer, "transposes this operation to 'passing in review all creatures' [60] or to having 'gone over and pondered . . . every aspect of the matter in question' [182]." So Ludolph could write: "Going through (*discurrentes*) the various places with a deep interior spirit, let them kiss or embrace the spot where they have learned that the gentle Jesus stood or sat or performed some deed." Ignatius himself will feel and practice the same reverence, not only literally in his Jerusalem pilgrimage, but also in his preparation for a prayer period and within the prayer period itself.

Ignatius wanted every novice of the Society of Jesus to have an experiment of pilgrimage to test his vocation to the Society of Jesus. Pilgrimage for Ignatius, both in the spiritual life identified in the *Spiritual Exercises* and in the Jesuit life described in the *Constitutions of the Society of*

Jesus, is not the straight-line road implied by the Spanish word *caminar*, but rather in the messiness of travel suggested by the Spanish word *discurrir*. The destination is clear and set, and one finds heartfelt meaning on the way there. But it takes some "traveling around" to get there.

To be a pilgrim also had its penitential aspects. We have to be content with the food (or lack thereof), with the lodging (or none at all), and even with our travel companions (not necessarily people we would have chosen). Although Ignatius always held on to the pilgrimage idea for Jesuit life (the indifference to food and lodging, and so on), to be a pilgrim, above all, is to experience trust in the Lord. To be a pilgrim is to let ourselves be led by the Lord, all a part of our seeking and finding God.

A Way of Proceeding

We cannot forget that the Gospel of St. Mark (the acknowledged first of the Gospels to be written down) begins with a quote from Isaiah about sending "my messenger before you to prepare your way." Jesus' public-life journey to Jerusalem is especially significant in the narrative of Luke's Gospel. And, of course, in the Acts of the Apostles, we know that the Christian community was called "the People of the Way." And so the notion of journey, which is present in many religious traditions, has a most important place in Christianity. Ignatius further refines its role in being a Christian by identifying the Jesuit Constitutions as a "way of proceeding." He knew that the Jesuit itinerant life could never be embraced by rules; he presumed that Jesuits would internalize in their formation a way of proceeding inherent to Jesuit life. In an analogous way, I believe that Ignatian spirituality finds such a wide audience because people internalize it as a "way of proceeding" in their spiritual life.

Returning to the word *pilgrimage*, we know that pilgrimage is also a major idea for many religious traditions, such as Muslims in their desire to make a journey to Mecca, and Hindus in their desire to come and bathe in the Ganges river. The whole medieval tradition of the famous four pilgrimage sites (Rome, Jerusalem, Canterbury, and Santiago de Compostello) still has its appeal in our own time. Of course, we have come to add Lourdes and Fatima and a number of other places associated with holy people.

Being a pilgrim, then, is a rich part of Ignatian spirituality. It is a spirituality that stresses we are always "finding our way." We need to stay alert to the lead of God in our life. We need to be always seeking and so finding, to be noting where God is acting, to be imagining how we are involved. That is all being part of a pilgrim identity.

Let us pray through the intercession of Ignatius that we can learn what it means to be a pilgrim. Let us be grateful that Ignatian spirituality gives us a way of proceeding in our following Jesus—what it means for us to follow Jesus.

Ignatian Ministry:
Working with Jesus in the Vineyard

Many of us are familiar with the military imagery used by St. Ignatius Loyola in the Call of the King meditation in the *Spiritual Exercises*. It is of the risen Christ giving a personal call to each man, woman, and child to be with him, to suffer with him, and to join him in the continuing struggle to achieve the kingdom of God. He also invites us to enjoy the victory he has already achieved through his resurrection. Ignatius also uses the image of a war to be won in the later meditation called the Two Standards, where "standards" denotes battle flags, one belonging to Lucifer and another to Christ. He even refers to Jesus as our Commander-in-chief.

60

Over the centuries, many have found the image of the battlefield, the challenging recruitment talk by Jesus, and the model response of the great-souled person to be the inspiration of their own vocation. Others, especially in recent times, have found the military imagery off-putting. Ignatius himself moved away from this more youthful, idealized imagery of chivalry (still with scripture roots, especially in St. Paul) to the gospel model of workers in the vineyard. When Ignatius set out to write the *Constitutions* for his newly church-approved Society of Jesus, he entitled the seventh part "The Distribution of the Incorporated Members in Christ's Vineyard and Their Relations There with Their Neighbor."

Ignatius uses the vineyard image, but he makes no references to a specific scripture text. The commonly understood reference is in the Gospel of St. Matthew. It begins:

> The reign of God is like the case of the owner of an estate who went out at dawn to hire workmen for his vineyard. After reaching an agreement with them for the usual daily wage, he sent them out to his vineyard. He came out about midmorning and saw other men standing around the marketplace without work, so he said to them, "You too go along to my vineyard and I will pay you whatever is fair." At that they went away. He came out again around noon and mid afternoon and did the same. Finally, going out in late afternoon he found still others standing around. To these he said, "Why have you been standing here idle all day?" "No one has hired us," they told him. He said, "You go to the vineyard too." (Mt 20:1-7)

The rest of the parable deals with the distribution of wages at the end of the day. When the workers discover that all will receive the same pay, the group that was hired in the morning complains about working in the heat of the day. The master replies that they agreed to the wage when hired. He challenges them about how they can question him about how he shows his generosity. If we approach this parable with our ideas of hourly

61

wages, it doesn't make much sense, and confirms an image of a demanding God who plays the game of life by his own rules.

Even when we approach the vineyard image through the lens of Ignatian usage, we need to accommodate the parable to the context of church mission. The vineyard is the symbol of God's creation, God's world. The vineyard is a place where things grow and produce. God, like the master, seeks out people to work with God in bringing about the kingdom of heaven or the reign of God. God continues to seek out people throughout the centuries; he calls people young in life and late in life to a special mission in working with God. This invitation, call, or vocation is always initiated by God—a gift to us. And we freely respond. The results (the wages) for those serving God early in life or later in life are the same— intimacy (being with Jesus) and life fulfillment (working with Jesus). But our relationship with God is not in terms of wages or pay; we are responding to God's love with our love. To work in the vineyard is to communicate with God (the Ignatian *comunicar*), and so we "share" with God in his coming of the kingdom. This is our prayer in every Our Father—thy kingdom come.

Helping

The image of God calling and sending us into the vineyard is at once an image of mission and ministry. In his consideration of ministry, Ignatius uses the active Spanish verb *ayudar*. We know that the word *ministry* is related to the verb "to minister, to serve." Ignatius extends this idea with his use of *ayudar*, a simple word meaning "to help." For example, the director in the Exercises retreat is always described as a "helper." The progress of the retreat is measured by "what helps." In the *Constitutions of the Society*, mission is described so

broadly in terms of ministries that we are forced to conclude that, if you were to ask what do Jesuits do, the
most honest response would be "we try to be helpful."

If we think of ourselves as being called by God to a
ministry, we are not frightened by the notion if we consider ourselves as simply trying to be "of help." Helping
does not require any academic degrees; in fact, one can
have lots of education or almost none. Helping does not
require any specific age range; you can be helpful at a
very young age and at a very old age. This helping relationship puts us alongside God, who is the One who
helps, the One who serves, the One who works, the One
who gifts, even in calling us to help. And so, in responding to the call to minister or to help, we must recognize
that we are also responding to the call to a new intimacy
with God.

Ministers or helpers are invited to be people of
prayer—they need to spend quality time with God. Then,
in the actual ministering or helping (whatever shape such
help takes), the minister or helper is able to relax because
he or she is only helping God, working alongside God.
Since God invites so many to help or minister, a helper
or minister expects that he or she will be working alongside others, also called by God. And so cooperation,
working with others, colleagueship, is an essential part
of being in God's vineyard. Sometimes, perhaps, like the
workers in the vineyard, we feel inclined to complain
about these colleagues of ours—they don't work as hard,
they are latecomers and take all the glory, they get the
recognition and we don't—and God needs to remind us
that we all are his helpers, by call, by grace, by gift.

Ignatius's gift of identifying our ministry always as
helping is the least threatening way of understanding
that God calls us to minister to one another. Perhaps we
would do well to pray about our role as ministers. We

could read slowly and reflect on the gospel passage of the vineyard from Matthew 20:1-16. We also might reflect on the passage from Mark 6:34-44 about Jesus feeding the 5000, and paying special attention to his question, "How many loaves have you?" It is a story about our helping relationship in bringing about the kingdom.

64

Ignatian Mission:
One Who Is Sent

Today in Catholic institutions such as schools and hospitals we often use the combined expression "mission and ministry." If ministry refers more to the "helping" in whatever way, then "mission" points to the "big picture," the more long-range goal, the continuity of effort. *Mission* in the root meaning of the word comes from the Latin *mitto*, which means " I send." So to be on mission is "to be sent."

In our Christian context, one does not give oneself a mission. Mission comes from another. We know that Jesus in the Gospel of St. John identifies himself as "the one who is sent." He has no words, no deeds of his own; what he says and what he does are always at the behest of

God the Father. When the Gospel records that he called his disciples together and selected twelve, he gave them the name Apostles. The word *apostle* indicates again "one who is sent."

In the *Constitutions of the Society of Jesus*, Ignatius took up the notion of the mission of the Jesuits in a chapter entitled "The Distribution of the Incorporated Members in Christ's Vineyard and Their Relations There with Their Neighbor." The vineyard image includes the owner taking the initiative to seek out workers for his vineyard. The owner makes his search for workers a number of times from dawn to late afternoon. Jesus emphasizes the owner and his call to work in the parable, just as God always is the one who calls us to our mission. Though God is always the origin of divine mission, our personal mission in life is ordinarily mediated through other human beings.

Listening

For Jesuits, the vow of obedience is particularly focused in terms of missioning. In order for a Jesuit to be missioned, there is always the process of discernment on the part of the individual and on the part of the superior, and only then is there the proper exercise of the vow of obedience. Both discernment and obedience demand a listening. As we listen to God, we seem to become aware of inclinations, drawings, that appear to come from deep within us. We often cannot explain why we feel so drawn, only that we cannot deny it. So in Christian life just as in religious life, the first source of a missioning is from God, and missioning, just like ministry, demands that we be people who pray, that is, be attuned to God. Where missioning comes concretely from a superior in religious life, it appears that missioning is confirmed for most Christians by one other person or by a special group—for example, sometimes by a spouse, sometimes by a spiritual director, sometimes by our prayer group or some kind of small community sharing.

A Focused Passion

There is a recent document of the Christian Life Community that describes mission as "focused passion." What does it mean for us to be "on mission"? It means our passion is focused. What a mission in life gives us is an excitement, an enthusiasm, an élan. It stems from and at the same time is centered on the mission we have. When Jesus says "I have come to light a fire on the earth; how I wish the blaze were ignited!" he is speaking with a focused passion; he is speaking of his mission. Dedication, a focused passion, then, is a necessary ingredient of mission.

How do we relate *having a mission* and *being a missionary*? St. Francis Xavier, early companion and close friend of Ignatius Loyola, is the symbol of *being a missionary*. Although we may have a personal mission in life, we don't earn the title "missionary," like Xavier, do we? Today, we acknowledge that the word *missionary* cannot be restricted only to those sent to evangelize in countries or cultures not their own. In fact, mission cannot be defined by geography, especially in our globalized world. Mission is not driven just by the zeal to expand the boundaries of the church—grateful as we are to the Xaviers and Cabrinis of the past and the present. To be missionary, however, does call us all to step out beyond the boundaries of our fears and our traditions and our cultures.

67

In the imagery of the vineyard, Ignatius draws upon Jesus' parable to indicate how Jesus has extended his mission to us all, who are missionary in our very baptismal being. Just as Jesus describes himself as "the one who is sent," so through the call of God the Father he sends us to proclaim the reign of God (close around us) and to make people aware of the nearness of a saving, loving God. Whatever form or shape our personal mission takes, we realize that our mission today must be exercised in the way we live and deal with others. Jesus images for us the way that God respects and dialogues with us human beings. Only with such dialogue and respect can we make ourselves one with God's mission.

Mission and ministry, integral to our being Christian, are also essential aspects of an Ignatian spirituality. We know that mission and ministry involve our hearts. They involve a total response from our person. Not only do we believe in what we are about, but we also have passion about it, a focused passion, and so we find ourselves "on mission." By living our Ignatian spirituality we are missionaries who delight in just being a helper.

As a help for our reflection and prayer, we can read the passage from Matthew 28:1-10, where the women on Easter morning are given a mission and a ministry twice over—from an angel and from Jesus. We might also find helpful the passage from John 20:11-18, where Mary Magdalen earns the title of "first apostle"—the one on mission from Jesus with a ministry to his disciples.

Mission and ministry: the Ignatian vocation of being a helper, by God's invitation and by others' direction and support, sent to our brothers and sisters.

Ignatian Spirituality and Educating: Visions

Being an educator in relation to Ignatian spirituality is like fitting a hand into a glove. There are some obvious factors, such as Ignatius Loyola and the original founding group of the Jesuit order all being graduate students together at the University of Paris in 1534. There is the historical reality that Jesuits very early on became identified through their schools and colleges as the "schoolmasters of Europe." A factor that is not often emphasized is that Ignatian spirituality is unique among the church spiritualities to be rooted in an exercise book. Exercise books have long been identified as an important educational tool.

Ignatius the Student

Ignatius Loyola describes his own way of growing in the spiritual life as if God were the schoolmaster and he the student. Towards the last years of his life, with pressure from his Jesuit companions, Ignatius dictated an account of his life that has come to be known as his *Autobiography*. In this book, when he refers to God teaching him during an intense spiritual period while he was living in Manresa, Spain, he identifies this action particularly with five lessons. The lessons all seem to deal with rather extraordinary experiences, ones that we might designate by the word *mystical*. But these lessons and many others that Ignatius learned become an integral part of his spirituality found in his *Spiritual Exercises*.

As teachers, we share knowledge. But more importantly we try to impart some notion of vision. By *vision* I mean to include "seeing the big picture," "presenting a wider context," or "setting forth an ideal." I am coming down on the side of opinion that values are necessarily a part of vision. And so we willy-nilly share some values by the vision we impart. Finally, as the mark of a good teacher, we present strategies, that is, ways of trying to make the visions and values a part of our way of living. Preachers and teachers both need to question themselves: preachers should ask themselves whether they have given any ways or means by which the people here in church can integrate the message into their lives and can live or act differently (many of us, being the recipients of the Sunday homily or sermon, are sadly aware that the question has not seemed to enter the preacher's mind). But to bring the same question home from preachers to us teachers, teachers, too, when teaching the material, should ask themselves whether they have given the ways or means by which these people in the classroom can integrate the matter into their previous knowledge and can call it "their own" or can work with it or do it.

Ignatius the Teacher

Ignatius's retreat manual, *Spiritual Exercises*, has all these elements of good teaching: presenting vision, imparting values, and suggesting strategies that will help the visions and values to become our own. Ignatius sets out to educate the heart, but he knows that the mind must necessarily be affected. We teachers more designedly desire to educate the mind, but we need to acknowledge that we do affect hearts too. I want to share with you one way of looking at Ignatius's vision, values, and strategies as I find them in his Exercises book in order to stir your own creativity and stimulate your own efforts as teachers of both minds and hearts.

Visions

We often say, "I won't believe it until I see it." But Ignatius challenges us with an alternate statement: When we believe it, we will see it. Vision controls our perception. And perception—how we perceive a person or a situation—controls our reality. The Jesuit paleontologist, Pierre Teilhard de Chardin, says, in a stark and striking way, in his book *The Phenomenon of Man*, that "the whole of life lies in that verb *seeing*." Vision is what Ignatius Loyola wants first to share with us, but we must acknowledge that he believed (he lived in a faith culture and God taught him) and so he saw.

Ignatius lived in a culture of faith. He is a born and bred Catholic, living in sixteenth-century Spain. God came into the life of this man, teaching him how to see as he never saw before. This way of seeing gave him his perspective on life. He took notes, and his notes became a book called *Spiritual Exercises*. Through his Spiritual Exercises, Ignatius wants to enter us into a vision that will give us a new way of perceiving our world.

Ignatius shares with us three visions—all dealing with

God. They really are the same vision, but we are look-ing at the same reality through different prisms. I will describe the three visions as 1) a life vision: what is life all about? 2) a work vision: what is our work or activity all about? and 3) a love vision: what is love all about? Let me briefly describe each of these visions.

A Life Vision

The first vision I have called "a life vision." This first vision that Ignatius presents is titled in the Exercises "The Principle and Foundation." Ignatius understands it as the basic vision we all need to have a sense of meaning for our lives. What is life all about? God is a God of life. God creates to give life. All the gifts that our created world represents are meant to give life and so help us to come to know God, the Giver of all good gifts, the Giver of life. For our part, we have a responsibility to choose among the gifts those that truly give us life and help us to know and respond to God in gratitude and love. That's what life is all about. We learn from God the meaning of our life.

A Work Vision

The second vision I have called "a work vision." What is work, human activity, all about? Why do we do what we do? The Ignatian title in the Exercises for this vision is "The Call of the King." For Ignatius, the vision is one of Jesus inviting every man, woman, and child, to be with him in the work of the kingdom of God or the reign of God. It is true that we pray, as Jesus taught us, "Thy kingdom come" every time we pray the Our Father. But prayer, though a priority, is not enough. God—Jesus—stoops down, as it were, and calls us to be participants in God's bringing this kingdom to fulfillment. It is a famil-iar Christian vision because St. Paul in his letters to the early churches echoes this call of Jesus for our participa-

tion in the coming of the reign of God. If we see ourselves with Christ in every activity, in all our works, our
prayers, our sufferings, we then have a vision of the eternal worth of everything we do. It is all part of that coming of the kingdom. What we do in our lifetime makes a
difference—*that* is a divine perspective. We learn from
God the value of all that we do. We are working with
God.

A Love Vision

The third vision that Ignatius presents I have called
"a love vision." Ignatius describes love in terms of two
activities: 1) love is shown more in deeds than in words,
and 2) love is a sharing between the two parties.
Comunicar is the Spanish word chosen by Ignatius: a
choice expression which is a wonderful reverse of the
first characteristic of love, saying that love is more about
deeds than *words*. By his choice of *comunicar*, Ignatius
indicates that lovers in their sharing are always *communicating*. He then presents the vision that God is not just
a Giver of gifts, but God is always trying to communicate
with us. Jesus, God-with-us, not only is our Savior and
Redeemer, but he also shares with us his very work for
our world. Like any lover, God is always working with us
and with God's world because that is the meaning of
love. In fact, there are no limits to the ways that God
pours forth his love—even if we try to kill this love by
crucifying Jesus on a cross or in whatever ways today we
personally may try to kill off God's love in our lives. And
from looking at the ways God loves, Ignatius raises the
question: What is love about for us? How do we go about
loving? How do we show our love for God, for ourselves,
for others, and for our world? Do we take our cue about
loving from God, who sets no limits? We learn from
God how to love.

Briefly, then, this is the vision that Ignatius wants us to enter into: a life vision, a work vision, and a love vision. Each vision in its own way gives us a perspective of "what it's all about."

74

Ignatian Spirituality and Educating: Values

Visions imply values. Ignatius spells out certain values that flow from the visions of life, of work, and of love (the lessons) that God has taught him. I might sum them up as follows: 1) what gives value to who we are? 2) what is the value in making decisions? And 3) what is the deepest value of our faith life?

Identity Values

In the Ignatian Exercises, the first value piece is titled "The Two Standards." Standards refer to the battle flags which identify the different forces. What flag shows our loyalty? What flag do we fight under? Ignatius points out that the values we observe indicate what flag we embrace. We can easily enough identify ourselves as Christian, but the values that we live betray often a different affiliation. And so Ignatius mentions certain evident values (values that are the apparent good in most cultures over the ages) such as the values of being wealthy, the value of being successful, the value of being important or a celebrity, the value of a great name or reputation. What gives us our worth? How do we value ourselves? People often take their identity, their worth, from their wealth, their fame, their success, even their education. Their very identity—their personal value— can get swallowed up in these goods. Ignatius then observes the values that Jesus proposes in the Gospels, and he finds countervalues to what the world or various cultures love and embrace. Can we come to understand and accept the values of Christ as the ones that give real meaning to our life? It is a hard struggle to understand and accept Christ's values in the face of our nation's or our culture's values. But for us the struggle is all-important. Christ's values make life meaningful because they acknowledge the basic value of our identity as sons and daughters of God. *There* is our real worth; it is God's gift, and no one can take it from us. It is the value that is the principle and foundation of our living. Jesus knew his identity as Son; sure, he was poor because everything was gift from God his Father. To us Jesus offers the surety of that same identity. We possess a value that no one can take from us. All other values can only flow from and be relative to this basic, fundamental value, the value of who we are, by God's grace.

Decision Values

The second value piece is titled "Three Kinds of People," and in this consideration Ignatius enters us into the question "What is the value in making decisions?" In his own life, Ignatius struggles with decisions. In fact, he had a kind of scrupulous personality that often tended to second-guess or third-guess himself. He met so many people who wanted to do some good things or desired to make a change, and nothing ever came of it. So Ignatius proposes a "case study" model for our way of appreciating the value of decision making. He has us consider one group of people who have all kinds of good intentions, but they die before they do anything about them. A second group of people will do various things to change or to right themselves, but they never do the one thing necessary since all they really want is half measures or compromise. A third group of people may not know immediately what they should do, but they stand ready, with ears and eyes open, to respond full-heartedly to the lead of God in their lives. As scripture says, "life is choice," and our lives have little value unless they are lived decisively. "Ready and willing" marks the value of making decisions.

Faith Values

A third value piece is titled "The Three Degrees of Humility" in the Exercises. Ignatius goes to the heart of the matter as we live our faith. He raises the question: How close in love would we want God to draw us? Using specifically the example of Jesus in his rejection by others and in his suffering and death on the cross, Ignatius has us consider what value we place on our "imitating" or "following" Jesus. It is a faith-value question, asking us to value our relationship with God. What is the deepest value of our faith? The deepest values of our faith must center on the ONE value—the closeness of our friendship with Jesus.

So Ignatius has presented us with a vision three times over and now reflections about values in three instances— values about identity, values about choice, and values about our faith relationship. We can pinpoint or name the occasions of these Ignatian visions and values as they appear in the Exercises. We are challenged to live them.

Ignatian Spirituality and Educating: Strategies

Pervasively, throughout the Exercises, we find Ignatius proposing strategies that hopefully will allow us to begin claiming the visions of life, of work, and of love and the values of identity, of decision, and of faith as our own. Let me identify five strategies and briefly describe them.

Heart Exercises

The first strategy I believe that Ignatius gives us fits right into the health-fitness emphasis in our country today. Ignatius compares spiritual exercises to physical exercises in their variety, first of all, but more comprehensively in terms of their necessity for health and wholeness.

If we want to be people of vision and of values, we must exercises ourselves. Ignatius would say that just as we acknowledge the necessity of exercises for the body, so too we must acknowledge the necessity of exercises for the heart. The first strategy is our effort and work at being spiritually healthy through heart exercises. He tries to make us aware that the exercises for the heart are many, and likely we are doing some. Heart exercises deal with all the acts and actions that releate us to God. But he has now drawn our attention to their importance, and he will continue to highlight some particular ones as he names other strategies in the course of the Exercises.

Examen

The second strategy Ignatius calls *examen*, a shortened form of the word *examination*. Examen is the Ignatian way of pointing to Socrates' maxim that "the unexamined life is not worth living." Ignatius would have us take short periods of time to reflect on our day, reflect on how we did something, and note God's presence or absence, and thank God or ask pardon. Examen is the essential Ignatian reflective strategy.

Ignatian Contemplation

The third strategy for Ignatius is prayer. Ignatius was very respectful of a person's way of praying. Throughout the Exercises book, he does offer some commonsense helps to pray. But only one prayer form has come to bear his name. It is called Ignatian contemplation. Ignatian contemplation describes a way of entering into the Gospels—scene by scene—and be present to Jesus and the other people in the scene, look at them and observe them, hear what they say, and watch what they do. It was the Ignatian strategy to come to know Jesus—a kind of personal knowledge that cannot be the fruit of any academic scripture study. Ignatius did not want us to hear Christ's words, "I never really knew you." So his strategy in prayer was a contemplation that allowed us to live with Jesus.

79

Discernment

A fourth strategy is the Ignatian helps for discernment and decision making. Much has been written on discernment, especially in recent times. Let me simply describe discernment as "a lover's sensitivity." People who love each other very much have a way of knowing how to anticipate needs or desires of the other. They easily read the other's face, listen to the voice inflection, and watch the way of walking with shoulders hunched. It is a lover's sensitivity that provides an avenue of knowledge. From contemplation, a prayer way of living with Christ, Ignatius hopes to engender in us a lover's sensitivity. In other words, for Ignatius, discernment is not so much a matter of the head, as it is the product of prayer—a way of knowing and even coming to a decision because of our lover's sensitivity. The decision is discerned because it is made with a lover's sensitivity.

Guidelines

A fifth strategy comes from observing the way Ignatius provides *reglas*—not *rules* (a common translation), but *guidelines*. From his own experience and from trying to be helpful to others, Ignatius came to know the advantage of setting down for oneself some guidelines, especially for ways of carrying out some work or ministry. Guidelines can be helpful especially in stressful or crisis-like situations. They can also keep us alert when we may feel the tendency to be bored or lethargic. Guidelines also make it easy for us to examine ourselves. And so guidelines become a helpful strategy for living a life of consistent integrity.

Ignatius, then, gives us visions, values, and strategies—all part of good teaching. Though he was formed in a Catholic culture, still he felt that God it was who taught him the way of visioning that he shares with us, the kinds of value articulation that he calls to our attention, and even the strategies—commonplace enough, but so effective that we can integrate them and claim these visions and values as our own.

Educating Today

Ignatius was the holy genius who wrote the book *Spiritual Exercises*. But each one of us who has made an Ignatian retreat has made the book our own—and that is what Ignatius intended. He provides only the exercises; we provide by means of our own life history the content or textbook. Ignatius rejoiced that he could help provide us with ways of visioning and articulations of values that we could claim as our own.

I hope that, in some analogous way, each of us can arrive at a way of educating and influencing students in an Ignatian manner. We may be inspired by the visions Ignatius presents to us; we may even have made them our own. But as teachers, what Ignatius teaches us is that we, each in our own way, must present a vision. The Christian values that Ignatius challenges us with may well be integral to our living. But as teachers, what Ignatius teaches us is that we need to make ourselves aware of the values we impart. Then, like Ignatius, we too can rejoice, not that our students think like us or know what we know, but that somehow we have shared with them visions and values and have provided them with some means—some strategies—that the ways of visioning and the articulations of values they claim *are* truly theirs, that they *own* them for themselves. Then we teachers will have been for our students an embodiment of an Ignatian exercise book.

Ignatian education prides itself on the phrase of educating "men and women for others." Let us also be proud and rejoice to say that by the way we educate we send forth men and women of vision and of values.

81

— ❦ —

Prayer to God our Teacher

Teach us, O God, to serve you as you deserve; to give and not to count the cost; to fight and not to notice the wounds; to toil and not to look for rest; to labor and not to ask for any reward, except that of knowing that we do your will through Jesus Christ our Lord.

Ignatius Loyola

82